THE ART OF THE
NATIONAL
PARKS

PARK-LOVER'S
JOURNAL

THE ART OF THE
NATIONAL
PARKS

PARK-LOVER'S
JOURNAL

BY *Fifty-Nine Parks*

EARTH AWARE

SAN RAFAEL · LOS ANGELES · LONDON

01. ACADIA (ME)	09. CANYONLANDS (UT)	17. DENALI (AK)	25. GRAND TETON (WY)
02. AMERICAN SAMOA	10. CAPITOL REEF (UT)	18. DRY TORTUGAS (FL)	26. GREAT BASIN (NV)
03. ARCHES (UT)	11. CARLSBAD CAVERNS (NM)	19. EVERGLADES (FL)	27. GREAT SAND DUNES (CO)
04. BADLANDS (SD)	12. CHANNEL ISLANDS (CA)	20. GATES OF THE ARCTIC (AK)	28. GREAT SMOKY MTNS. (TN/NC)
05. BIG BEND (TX)	13. CONGAREE (SC)	21. GATEWAY ARCH (MO)	29. GUADALUPE MTNS. (TX)
06. BISCAYNE (FL)	14. CRATER LAKE (OR)	22. GLACIER (MT)	30. HALEAKALA (HI)
07. BLACK CANYON (CO)	15. CUYAHOGA VALLEY (OH)	23. GLACIER BAY (AK)	31. HAWAII VOLCANOES (HI)
08. BRYCE CANYON (UT)	16. DEATH VALLEY (CA/NV)	24. GRAND CANYON (AZ)	32. HOT SPRINGS (AR)

NAL PARKS
STATES OF AMERICA

Fifty-Nine Parks
59PARKS.NET

33. INDIANA DUNES (IN)
34. ISLE ROYALE (MI)
35. JOSHUA TREE (CA)
36. KATMAI (AK)
37. KENAI FJORDS (AK)
38. KINGS CANYON (CA)
39. KOBUK VALLEY (AK)
40. LAKE CLARK (AK)

41. LASSEN VOLCANIC (CA)
42. MAMMOTH CAVE (KY)
43. MESA VERDE (CO)
44. MOUNT RAINIER (WA)
45. NEW RIVER GORGE (WV)
46. NORTH CASCADES (WA)
47. OLYMPIC (WA)
48. PETRIFIED FOREST (AZ)

49. PINNACLES (CA)
50. REDWOOD (CA)
51. ROCKY MOUNTAIN (CO)
52. SAGUARO (AZ)
53. SEQUOIA (CA)
54. SHENANDOAH (VA)
55. THEODORE ROOSEVELT (ND)
56. VIRGIN ISLANDS

57. VOYAGEURS (MN)
58. WHITE SANDS (NM)
59. WIND CAVE (SD)
60. WRANGELL-ST. ELIAS (AK)
61. YELLOWSTONE (WY/MT/ID)
62. YOSEMITE (CA)
63. ZION (UT)

ACADIA NATIONAL PARK

ESTABLISHED 1916

ACADIA NATIONAL PARK

first became a national monument in 1916. It is known for its jagged Atlantic coastline, sprawling woodlands, and scattered lakes that stretch across 47,000 acres.

DATE OF VISIT _____

WHERE DID YOU STAY? _____

_____

_____

_____

WHO WERE YOU WITH? _____

_____

_____

_____

WHAT DID YOU DO? _____

_____

_____

_____

WHAT DID YOU SEE? _____

_____

_____

_____

FLORA _____

_____

FAUNA _____

_____

FAVORITE MEMORIES _____

_____

_____

_____

_____

_____

_____

ATTRACTIONS VISITED

☐ Champlain Mountain & Beehive Loop Trail

☐ Cadillac Mountain

☐ Sand Beach

☐ Thunder Hole

☐ Bar Harbor

MAMMOTH CAVE NATIONAL PARK

is composed of two vastly different landscapes:
the lush Kentucky countryside and the dark
caverns beneath.

DATE OF VISIT _____

WHERE DID YOU STAY? _____

_____

_____

_____

WHO WERE YOU WITH? _____

_____

_____

_____

WHAT DID YOU DO? _____

_____

_____

_____

WHAT DID YOU SEE? _____

_____

_____

FLORA _____

FAUNA _____

FAVORITE MEMORIES _____

_____

_____

_____

_____

_____

_____

VISITOR'S STAMP

ATTRACTIONS VISITED

- ☐ Mammoth Cave
- ☐ Fat Man's Misery
- ☐ Cedar Sink Trail
- ☐ Echo River
- ☐ Wild Cave Tour

| STATE: KENTUCKY | ARTIST: NICOLAS DELORT |

MAMMOTH CAVE NATIONAL PARK

ESTABLISHED 1941

SHENANDOAH NATIONAL PARK

ESTABLISHED 1935

SHENANDOAH NATIONAL PARK

offers scenic views of the Blue Ridge Mountains and the rolling hills of the countryside, just 75 miles from Washington D.C. in northern Virginia.

DATE OF VISIT _____

WHERE DID YOU STAY? _____

_____

_____

WHO WERE YOU WITH? _____

_____

_____

WHAT DID YOU DO? _____

_____

_____

_____

WHAT DID YOU SEE? _____

_____

_____

FLORA _____

FAUNA _____

FAVORITE MEMORIES _____

_____

_____

_____

_____

_____

_____

ATTRACTIONS VISITED

- ☐ Mary's Rock Summit Trail
- ☐ Dark Hollow Falls
- ☐ Bearfence Mountain
- ☐ Skyline Drive
- ☐ Skyland Mountain

NEW RIVER GORGE NATIONAL PARK

includes more than 72,000 acres of land and 53 miles of free-flowing river. It offers a plethora of activities, including rock climbing, hiking, biking, camping, and fishing.

DATE OF VISIT _____

WHERE DID YOU STAY? _____
_____

WHO WERE YOU WITH? _____
_____
_____
_____

ATTRACTIONS VISITED

- [ ] New River Gorge Bridge
- [ ] Endless Wall Trail
- [ ] Sandstone Falls
- [ ] Whitewater Rafting – Lower Gorge
- [ ] Grandview Outlook

WHAT DID YOU DO? _____
_____
_____
_____

WHAT DID YOU SEE? _____
_____
_____

FLORA _____

FAUNA _____

FAVORITE MEMORIES _____
_____
_____
_____
_____
_____
_____
_____

NEW RIVER GORGE NATIONAL PARK

ESTABLISHED 2020

GREAT SMOKY MOUNTAINS NATIONAL PARK

ESTABLISHED 1934

GREAT SMOKY MOUNTAINS NATIONAL PARK

is aptly named for its perpetual fog. The most visited national park in the United States, the Smokies are filled with wildflowers and waterfalls, bestriding Tennessee and North Carolina.

DATE OF VISIT _____

WHERE DID YOU STAY? _____
_____
_____

ATTRACTIONS VISITED
- ☐ Roaring Fork Motor Nature Trail
- ☐ Cades Cove
- ☐ Clingmans Dome
- ☐ Laurel Falls
- ☐ Chimney Tops Trail

WHO WERE YOU WITH? _____
_____
_____

WHAT DID YOU DO? _____
_____
_____
_____

WHAT DID YOU SEE? _____
_____
_____

FLORA _____

FAUNA _____

FAVORITE MEMORIES _____
_____
_____
_____
_____
_____

CONGAREE NATIONAL PARK

is named for the river that flows through the park. It boasts some of the tallest trees in the eastern United States. This floodplain hardwood forest fosters astonishing biodiversity in central South Carolina.

DATE OF VISIT _____

WHERE DID YOU STAY? _____

_____

_____

ATTRACTIONS VISITED

☐ Boardwalk Loop
☐ Congaree River
☐ Weston Lake Loop
☐ Cedar Creek
☐ Oakridge Trail

WHO WERE YOU WITH? _____

_____

_____

_____

WHAT DID YOU DO? _____

_____

_____

_____

WHAT DID YOU SEE? _____

_____

_____

FLORA _____

FAUNA _____

FAVORITE MEMORIES _____

_____

_____

_____

_____

_____

_____

CONGAREE NATIONAL PARK

ESTABLISHED 2003

BISCAYNE NATIONAL PARK

ESTABLISHED 1980

BISCAYNE NATIONAL PARK

is one of the largest marine sanctuaries in the US National Parks system. Its thirty-five-mile-long lagoon shelters a plethora of endangered species between the tip of Florida and the Bahamas.

DATE OF VISIT _____

WHERE DID YOU STAY? _____

_____

_____

_____

WHO WERE YOU WITH? _____

_____

_____

WHAT DID YOU DO? _____

_____

_____

_____

WHAT DID YOU SEE? _____

_____

_____

FLORA _____

FAUNA _____

FAVORITE MEMORIES _____

_____

_____

_____

_____

_____

_____

ATTRACTIONS VISITED

☐ Boca Chita Key

☐ Elliott Key

☐ Adams Key

☐ Biscayne Birding Trail

☐ Jones Lagoon

DRY TORTUGAS NATIONAL PARK

is 99 percent water, save for a collection of tiny islands that are accessible only by boat or plane. It is home to incredible coral reefs, diverse sea creatures, and various bird life.

DATE OF VISIT _____

WHERE DID YOU STAY? _____

_____

_____

WHO WERE YOU WITH? _____

_____

_____

_____

ATTRACTIONS VISITED

☐ Fort Jefferson
☐ The Yankee Freedom Ferry
☐ Snorkeling the Moat Wall
☐ Windjammer Shipwreck
☐ Coral reefs

WHAT DID YOU DO? _____

_____

_____

_____

WHAT DID YOU SEE? _____

_____

_____

FLORA _____

FAUNA _____

FAVORITE MEMORIES _____

_____

_____

_____

_____

_____

_____

DRY TORTUGAS NATIONAL PARK

ESTABLISHED 1935

EVERGLADES NATIONAL PARK

ESTABLISHED 1947

EVERGLADES NATIONAL PARK

contains a mixture of ocean water from the Florida Bay
and the water of the Okeechobee River, creating swampy
forests that make up the largest tropical wilderness in
the United States.

DATE OF VISIT

WHERE DID YOU STAY?

WHO WERE YOU WITH?

WHAT DID YOU DO?

WHAT DID YOU SEE?

FLORA

FAUNA

FAVORITE MEMORIES

ATTRACTIONS VISITED

☐ Long Pine Key Nature Trail
☐ Shark Valley
☐ Anhinga Trail
☐ HM69 Nike Missile Base
☐ Nine Mile Pond Canoe Trail

VIRGIN ISLANDS NATIONAL PARK

encompasses nearly 15,000 acres of pristine beaches,
tropical forests, and vivid seascapes.

DATE OF VISIT _____

WHERE DID YOU STAY? _____

_____

_____

_____

WHO WERE YOU WITH? _____

_____

_____

_____

_____

WHAT DID YOU DO? _____

_____

_____

_____

WHAT DID YOU SEE? _____

_____

_____

FLORA _____

_____

FAUNA _____

_____

FAVORITE MEMORIES _____

_____

_____

_____

_____

_____

ATTRACTIONS VISITED

- ☐ Trunk Bay Beach
- ☐ Cinnamon Bay
- ☐ Waterlemon Cay
- ☐ Reef Bay Trail
- ☐ Coral Reef Underwater
  Park Trail

VIRGIN ISLANDS NATIONAL PARK

ESTABLISHED 1956

CUYAHOGA VALLEY NATIONAL PARK

ESTABLISHED 2000

CUYAHOGA VALLEY NATIONAL PARK

offers stunning views of Ohio's countryside. The
sinuous Cuyahoga River flows through the park's lush
woody floodplains, rolling and sprawling hills, and
winding ravines.

DATE OF VISIT _____

WHERE DID YOU STAY? _____

_____

_____

WHO WERE YOU WITH? _____

_____

_____

_____

WHAT DID YOU DO? _____

_____

_____

_____

WHAT DID YOU SEE? _____

_____

_____

FLORA _____

_____

FAUNA _____

_____

FAVORITE MEMORIES _____

_____

_____

_____

_____

_____

_____

ATTRACTIONS VISITED

- [ ] Cuyahoga Valley Scenic Railroad
- [ ] The Ledges Overlook
- [ ] Brandywine Falls
- [ ] Blue Hen Falls
- [ ] Tree Farm Trail

ISLE ROYALE NATIONAL PARK

is a forty-five-mile-long island of glacier-scarred volcanic rock. It is located deep in Michigan's Lake Superior—the most remote park in the contiguous United States.

DATE OF VISIT _____

WHERE DID YOU STAY? _____

_____

_____

WHO WERE YOU WITH? _____

_____

_____

_____

ATTRACTIONS VISITED

☐ Rock Harbor
☐ Scoville Point
☐ Greenstone Ridge Trail
☐ Rock Island Lighthouse
☐ Suzy's Cave

WHAT DID YOU DO? _____

_____

_____

_____

WHAT DID YOU SEE? _____

_____

_____

FLORA _____

_____

FAUNA _____

_____

FAVORITE MEMORIES _____

_____

_____

_____

_____

_____

_____

_____

ISLE ROYALE NATIONAL PARK

ESTABLISHED 1940

INDIANA DUNES NATIONAL PARK

ESTABLISHED 2019

INDIANA DUNES NATIONAL PARK

encompasses 15,000 acres of land and hugs 15 miles of Lake Michigan's shore. A diverse landscape, it includes sand dunes, prairies, wetlands, forests, swamps, bogs, marshes, and a river.

DATE OF VISIT _____

WHERE DID YOU STAY? _____

_____

_____

ATTRACTIONS VISITED
- ☐ Dune Succession Trail
- ☐ Paul H. Douglas Trail (Miller Woods)
- ☐ Mount Baldy & Beach
- ☐ Tremont Picnic Area
- ☐ Calumet Trail

WHO WERE YOU WITH? _____

_____

_____

_____

WHAT DID YOU DO? _____

_____

_____

_____

_____

WHAT DID YOU SEE? _____

_____

_____

_____

FLORA _____

_____

FAUNA _____

_____

FAVORITE MEMORIES _____

_____

_____

_____

_____

_____

_____

_____

GATEWAY ARCH NATIONAL PARK

is a 630-foot-high monument in St. Louis, Missouri, designed by architect Eero Saarinen and structural engineer Hannskarl Bandel in 1947. It is an emblem of US history, a symbol of westward expansion, and a reminder of the horrors of slavery.

DATE OF VISIT _____

WHERE DID YOU STAY? _____
_____
_____

WHO WERE YOU WITH? _____
_____

ATTRACTIONS VISITED

☐ Tram Ride to the Top
☐ The Old Courthouse
☐ The Museum at the Gateway Arch

WHAT DID YOU DO? _____
_____
_____

WHAT DID YOU SEE? _____
_____
_____

FLORA _____

FAUNA _____

FAVORITE MEMORIES _____
_____
_____
_____
_____
_____

GATEWAY ARCH NATIONAL PARK

HOT SPRINGS NATIONAL PARK

ESTABLISHED 1832

HOT SPRINGS NATIONAL PARK

contains 47 steaming, bubbling thermal springs that produce over 7,000 gallons of water a day. It is located in Arkansas's central Garland County.

DATE OF VISIT _____

WHERE DID YOU STAY? _____

_____

_____

_____

ATTRACTIONS VISITED

☐ Garvan Woodland Gardens

☐ Bathhouse Row

☐ Hotsprings Mountain

☐ West Mountain

☐ Sunset Trail

WHO WERE YOU WITH? _____

_____

_____

_____

WHAT DID YOU DO? _____

_____

_____

_____

WHAT DID YOU SEE? _____

_____

_____

FLORA _____

_____

FAUNA _____

_____

FAVORITE MEMORIES _____

_____

_____

_____

_____

_____

_____

VOYAGEURS NATIONAL PARK

is made up of more than 900 islands and features four
main lakes full of glinting, sapphire water: Rainy Lake,
Kabetogama Lake, Namakan Lake, and Sand Point Lake.

DATE OF VISIT _____

WHERE DID YOU STAY? _____

_____

_____

_____

WHO WERE YOU WITH? _____

_____

_____

_____

WHAT DID YOU DO? _____

_____

_____

_____

WHAT DID YOU SEE? _____

_____

_____

FLORA _____

FAUNA _____

FAVORITE MEMORIES _____

_____

_____

_____

_____

_____

_____

ATTRACTIONS VISITED

- [ ] Grassy Bay Cliffs
- [ ] Anderson Bay
- [ ] Kabetogama Peninsula
- [ ] Ellsworth Rock Gardens
- [ ] Beaver Pond Overlook

VOYAGEURS NATIONAL PARK

ESTABLISHED 1975

THEODORE ROOSEVELT NATIONAL PARK

ESTABLISHED 1978

THEODORE ROOSEVELT NATIONAL PARK

is teeming with wildlife and lush greenery. It's easy to
see how the raw natural beauty of this park inspired
Roosevelt to become one of the most outspoken and
powerful conservationists of all time.

DATE OF VISIT _____

WHERE DID YOU STAY? _____

_____

_____

WHO WERE YOU WITH? _____

_____

_____

_____

ATTRACTIONS VISITED

☐ Painted Canyon Overlook
☐ South Unit
☐ North Unit
☐ Petrified Forest Loop
☐ Oxbow Overlook

WHAT DID YOU DO? _____

_____

_____

_____

WHAT DID YOU SEE? _____

_____

_____

FLORA _____

FAUNA _____

FAVORITE MEMORIES _____

_____

_____

_____

_____

_____

_____

BADLANDS NATIONAL PARK

first became a national monument in 1939. Its pinnacles and eroded buttes were built up over millions of years of deposition, only to begin eroding 500,000 years ago from rivers and rainfall. Vultures, snakes, bison, pronghorns, and bighorn sheep roam freely.

DATE OF VISIT _____

WHERE DID YOU STAY? _____

_____

ATTRACTIONS VISITED

☐ Badlands Wall

☐ Notch Trail

WHO WERE YOU WITH? _____

☐ Pinnacles Overlook

_____

☐ Door Trail

_____

☐ Fossil Exhibit Trail

WHAT DID YOU DO? _____

_____

_____

_____

WHAT DID YOU SEE? _____

_____

_____

FLORA _____

FAUNA _____

FAVORITE MEMORIES _____

_____

_____

_____

_____

_____

_____

BADLANDS NATIONAL PARK

ESTABLISHED 1939

WIND CAVE NATIONAL PARK

ESTABLISHED 1903

WIND CAVES NATIONAL PARK

is considered a sacred place by the Lakota Sioux of
South Dakota, with over 149 miles of complex mazelike
passageways. Aboveground, bison, elk, and prairie dogs
roam across the largest mixed-grass prairie.

DATE OF VISIT _____

WHERE DID YOU STAY? _____

_____

_____

WHO WERE YOU WITH? _____

_____

_____

_____

WHAT DID YOU DO? _____

_____

_____

_____

WHAT DID YOU SEE? _____

_____

_____

FLORA _____

_____

FAUNA _____

_____

FAVORITE MEMORIES _____

_____

_____

_____

_____

_____

_____

ATTRACTIONS VISITED
- ☐ Rankin Ridge Nature Trail
- ☐ Elk Mountain Trail
- ☐ Prairie Vista
- ☐ Lookout Point
- ☐ Garden of Eden Cave Tour

GUADALUPE MOUNTAINS NATIONAL PARK

sits astride the path of a long-abandoned stagecoach route in the desert of West Texas. What seems at first like an endless desert is revealed to be a great myriad of ecosystems, from verdant forests to heaping sand dunes.

DATE OF VISIT _____

WHERE DID YOU STAY? _____

WHO WERE YOU WITH? _____

ATTRACTIONS VISITED

- [ ] Guadalupe Peak
- [ ] McKittrick Canyon
- [ ] Devil's Hall Trail
- [ ] Smith Spring
- [ ] El Capitan

WHAT DID YOU DO? _____

WHAT DID YOU SEE? _____

FLORA _____

FAUNA _____

FAVORITE MEMORIES _____

GUADALUPE MOUNTAINS NATIONAL PARK

ESTABLISHED 1972

BIG BEND NATIONAL PARK

ESTABLISHED 1944

BIG BEND NATIONAL PARK

stretches over 800,000 acres. Over the course of millions of years, the Rio Grande's mighty waters carved their way through the limestone walls of these towering canyons deep in Texas.

DATE OF VISIT _____

WHERE DID YOU STAY? _____

_____

WHO WERE YOU WITH? _____

_____

_____

_____

WHAT DID YOU DO? _____

_____

_____

_____

WHAT DID YOU SEE? _____

_____

_____

FLORA _____

FAUNA _____

FAVORITE MEMORIES _____

_____

_____

_____

_____

_____

_____

ATTRACTIONS VISITED

☐ Santa Elena Canyon
☐ Lost Mine Trail
☐ The Window Trail
☐ Ross Maxwell Scenic Drive
☐ Hot Springs Historic District

GRAND CANYON NATIONAL PARK

is one of the Seven Wonders of the World. It's a nearly two-million-square-mile gorge carved out by the incessant rush of the Colorado River.

DATE OF VISIT

WHERE DID YOU STAY?

WHO WERE YOU WITH?

WHAT DID YOU DO?

WHAT DID YOU SEE?

FLORA

FAUNA

FAVORITE MEMORIES

ATTRACTIONS VISITED
- [ ] Grand Canyon North or South Rim
- [ ] Bright Angel Trail
- [ ] South Kaibab Trail
- [ ] Mather Point
- [ ] Grandview Point

GRAND CANYON NATIONAL PARK

ESTABLISHED 1919

PETRIFIED FOREST NATIONAL PARK

ESTABLISHED 1962

PETRIFIED FOREST NATIONAL PARK

is a rich source of dinosaur bones and fossilized footprints from eons of natural fossilization. Millions of years ago, this place in Arizona was a swamp; now, all 220,000 acres of the forest are above 5,000 feet.

DATE OF VISIT _____

WHERE DID YOU STAY? _____

_____

_____

WHO WERE YOU WITH? _____

_____

_____

_____

WHAT DID YOU DO? _____

_____

_____

_____

WHAT DID YOU SEE? _____

_____

_____

FLORA _____

FAUNA _____

FAVORITE MEMORIES _____

_____

_____

_____

_____

_____

_____

ATTRACTIONS VISITED

☐ Painted Desert
☐ Blue Mesa
☐ Rainbow Forest
☐ Devil's Playground
☐ Crystal Forest Trail

SAGUARO NATIONAL PARK

is located in southeastern Arizona. It is the only place in the world where the eponymous saguaro grows, and 91,000 acres of mountains and desert are protected to preserve this iconic cactus.

DATE OF VISIT _____

WHERE DID YOU STAY? _____

_____

_____

WHO WERE YOU WITH? _____

_____

_____

WHAT DID YOU DO? _____

_____

_____

_____

WHAT DID YOU SEE? _____

_____

_____

FLORA _____

FAUNA _____

FAVORITE MEMORIES _____

_____

_____

_____

_____

_____

ATTRACTIONS VISITED

- ☐ Hope Camp and Ridgeview Trail
- ☐ King Canyon/ Gould Mine Loop
- ☐ Rincon Mountains
- ☐ Wasson Peak
- ☐ Arizona-Sonora Desert Museum

SAGUARO NATIONAL PARK

ESTABLISHED 1994

CARLSBAD CAVERNS NATIONAL PARK

ESTABLISHED 1930

CARLSBAD CAVERNS NATIONAL PARK

is located in southwestern New Mexico's Chihuahuan desert. It features 120 natural caves, numerous canyons, and one of the world's best-preserved fossilized reefs.

DATE OF VISIT _____

WHERE DID YOU STAY? _____

_____

_____

WHO WERE YOU WITH? _____

_____

_____

_____

WHAT DID YOU DO? _____

_____

_____

_____

WHAT DID YOU SEE? _____

_____

_____

FLORA _____

FAUNA _____

FAVORITE MEMORIES _____

_____

_____

_____

_____

_____

_____

VISITOR'S STAMP

ATTRACTIONS VISITED

☐ Big Room Cave
☐ King's Palace Cave
☐ Bottomless Pit
☐ Green Lake
☐ Slaughter Canyon Cave

WHITE SANDS NATIONAL PARK

encompasses more than 275 square miles of powdery dunes that stretch up to fifteen feet tall. Located in central New Mexico, rodents and reptiles live among desert succulents, cacti, and yuca.

DATE OF VISIT

WHERE DID YOU STAY?

WHO WERE YOU WITH?

ATTRACTIONS VISITED

- [ ] Interdune Boardwalk
- [ ] Dunes Life Nature Trail
- [ ] Alkali Flat Trailhead
- [ ] Lake Lucero
- [ ] Sledding on the dunes

WHAT DID YOU DO?

WHAT DID YOU SEE?

FLORA

FAUNA

FAVORITE MEMORIES

WHITE SANDS NATIONAL PARK

ESTABLISHED 2019

BLACK CANYON OF THE GUNNISON NATIONAL PARK

ESTABLISHED 1999

BLACK CANYON OF THE GUNNISON NATIONAL PARK

was formed more than two million years by the Gunnison River that runs through it. The colossal 2,000-foot-deep Black Canyon is the deepest, narrowest, and darkest canyon in the country.

DATE OF VISIT _____

WHERE DID YOU STAY? _____

_____

ATTRACTIONS VISITED

☐ North or South Rim Road

☐ Painted Wall

WHO WERE YOU WITH? _____

☐ Pulpit Rock Overlook

☐ Warner Point

_____

☐ Tomichi Point

_____

WHAT DID YOU DO? _____

_____

_____

_____

WHAT DID YOU SEE? _____

_____

_____

FLORA _____

FAUNA _____

FAVORITE MEMORIES _____

_____

_____

_____

_____

_____

_____

BRYCE CANYON NATIONAL PARK

of southern Utah has the highest concentration of hoodoos—mushroom-like rock formations—in the world. The 35,835-acre park also features a collection of natural amphitheaters with rocks of red, orange, and white.

DATE OF VISIT _____

WHERE DID YOU STAY? _____

_____

_____

ATTRACTIONS VISITED

☐ Queen's Garden Trail

☐ Sunset Point

WHO WERE YOU WITH? _____

☐ Navajo Trail

☐ Inspiration Point

_____

☐ Fairyland Loop

_____

WHAT DID YOU DO? _____

_____

_____

_____

_____

WHAT DID YOU SEE? _____

_____

_____

FLORA _____

_____

FAUNA _____

_____

FAVORITE MEMORIES _____

_____

_____

_____

_____

_____

_____

_____

_____

BRYCE CANYON NATIONAL PARK

ESTABLISHED 1928

GREAT SAND DUNES NATIONAL PARK

ESTABLISHED 2004

GREAT SAND DUNES NATIONAL PARK

contains over 30 square miles of mysterious and surreal sand dunes, some soaring as high as 750 feet. Trails lead to a varied landscape of snowy mountains, sand dunes, rich forests, and warm wetlands.

DATE OF VISIT _____

WHERE DID YOU STAY? _____

_____

_____

ATTRACTIONS VISITED

☐ Zapata Falls
☐ High Dune Trail
☐ Little Medano Creek
☐ Mount Herard

WHO WERE YOU WITH? _____

_____

_____

WHAT DID YOU DO? _____

_____

_____

_____

WHAT DID YOU SEE? _____

_____

_____

FLORA _____

_____

FAUNA _____

_____

FAVORITE MEMORIES _____

_____

_____

_____

_____

_____

_____

MESA VERDE NATIONAL PARK

is one of the best preserved archeological sites on Earth, with more than 600 cliff dwellings left behind by Ancestral Puebloans. It is uniquely located at the Four Corners of the United States—where Arizona meets Utah, New Mexico, and Colorado.

DATE OF VISIT _____

WHERE DID YOU STAY? _____

_____

_____

WHO WERE YOU WITH? _____

_____

_____

_____

ATTRACTIONS VISITED

☐ Cliff Palace

☐ Balcony House

☐ Petroglyph Point Trail

☐ Soda Canyon Overlook Trail

☐ Prater Ridge Trail

WHAT DID YOU DO? _____

_____

_____

_____

WHAT DID YOU SEE? _____

_____

_____

FLORA _____

_____

FAUNA _____

_____

FAVORITE MEMORIES _____

_____

_____

_____

_____

_____

_____

_____

_____

MESA VERDE NATIONAL PARK

ESTABLISHED 1906

ROCKY MOUNTAIN NATIONAL PARK

ESTABLISHED 1915

ROCKY MOUNTAIN NATIONAL PARK

contains some of the most treacherous paths
that settlers braved to get to the West. It spans
northern Colorado along the Continental Divide
with majestic peaks in every direction and wildlife
everywhere you look.

DATE OF VISIT _____

WHERE DID YOU STAY? _____

_____

_____

WHO WERE YOU WITH? _____

_____

_____

ATTRACTIONS VISITED

☐ Trail Ridge Road
☐ Emerald Lake Trail
☐ Bear Lake
☐ Alberta Falls
☐ Chapel on the Rock

WHAT DID YOU DO? _____

WHAT DID YOU SEE? _____

FLORA _____

FAUNA _____

FAVORITE MEMORIES _____

GRAND TETON NATIONAL PARK

has a mountain range that shoots up 7,000 feet high straight from the lowlands of the Jackson Hole valley. Hundreds of black bears and grizzly bears live here along with elk, pronghorns, beavers, moose, and bison.

DATE OF VISIT _____

WHERE DID YOU STAY? _____

_____

ATTRACTIONS VISITED
- [ ] Jenny Lake Trail
- [ ] Schwabacher Landing

WHO WERE YOU WITH? _____
- [ ] Jackson Lake
- [ ] Cascade Canyon Trail
_____
- [ ] Signal Mountain
_____ Summit Road

_____

WHAT DID YOU DO? _____

_____

_____

_____

WHAT DID YOU SEE? _____

_____

_____

FLORA _____

FAUNA _____

FAVORITE MEMORIES _____

_____

_____

_____

_____

_____

_____

GRAND TETON NATIONAL PARK

ESTABLISHED 1929

YELLOWSTONE NATIONAL PARK

ESTABLISHED 1872

YELLOWSTONE NATIONAL PARK

represents the American ideal. It has everything:
lakes, rivers, canyons, mountain ranges, forests,
wildlife, world-famous geothermal features, and even
a volcano, located in Wyoming, as well as some parts
of Montana and Idaho.

DATE OF VISIT _____

WHERE DID YOU STAY? _____

_____

_____

ATTRACTIONS VISITED

☐ Old Faithful Geyser

☐ Grand Prismatic Spring

WHO WERE YOU WITH? _____

☐ Mammoth Hot Springs

_____

☐ Artist Point

_____

☐ Mystic Falls Trail

WHAT DID YOU DO? _____

_____

_____

_____

WHAT DID YOU SEE? _____

_____

_____

FLORA _____

FAUNA _____

_____

FAVORITE MEMORIES _____

_____

_____

_____

_____

_____

_____

_____

GLACIER NATIONAL PARK

has jagged mountain peaks, alpine glaciers, and gushing waterfalls. While there were once 150 glaciers in the park, they have since dwindled down to fewer than 30— an important reminder of nature's impermanence.

DATE OF VISIT _____

WHERE DID YOU STAY? _____

_____

_____

WHO WERE YOU WITH? _____

_____

_____

_____

WHAT DID YOU DO? _____

_____

_____

_____

WHAT DID YOU SEE? _____

_____

_____

FLORA _____

FAUNA _____

FAVORITE MEMORIES _____

_____

_____

_____

_____

_____

_____

_____

ATTRACTIONS VISITED

- ☐ Going-to-the-Sun Road
- ☐ Grinnell Glacier
- ☐ Lake McDonald
- ☐ Avalanche Lake Trail
- ☐ Logan Pass

GLACIER NATIONAL PARK

ESTABLISHED 1910

DEATH VALLEY NATIONAL PARK

ESTABLISHED 1994

DEATH VALLEY NATIONAL PARK

is the lowest, driest, and hottest national park in the country. In the Great Basin and Mojave Desert, canyons, valleys, and mountains tower over swirling sand dunes, trickling salt flats, and haunting badlands.

DATE OF VISIT _____

WHERE DID YOU STAY? _____

_____

WHO WERE YOU WITH? _____

_____

_____

_____

WHAT DID YOU DO? _____

_____

_____

_____

WHAT DID YOU SEE? _____

_____

_____

_____

FLORA _____

_____

FAUNA _____

_____

FAVORITE MEMORIES _____

_____

_____

_____

_____

_____

_____

VISITOR'S STAMP

ATTRACTIONS VISITED

- ☐ Badwater Basin
- ☐ Zabriskie Point
- ☐ Dante's View
- ☐ Mesquite Flat Sand Dune
- ☐ Titus Canyon

JOSHUA TREE NATIONAL PARK

is most famous for the eponymous Joshua Tree, also known as the *Yucca brevifolia*. A certified Dark Sky Park, it is far enough from the light pollution of nearby cities for visitors to enjoy incredible stargazing.

DATE OF VISIT _____

WHERE DID YOU STAY? _____

_____

ATTRACTIONS VISITED

☐ Cholla Cactus Garden

WHO WERE YOU WITH? _____

☐ Arch Rock Nature Trail

_____

☐ Skull Rock

_____

☐ Hidden Valley

_____

☐ Keys View

WHAT DID YOU DO? _____

_____

_____

_____

WHAT DID YOU SEE? _____

_____

_____

FLORA _____

_____

FAUNA _____

_____

FAVORITE MEMORIES _____

_____

_____

_____

_____

_____

_____

JOSHUA TREE NATIONAL PARK

ESTABLISHED 1994

KINGS CANYON NATIONAL PARK

ESTABLISHED 1940

KINGS CANYON NATIONAL PARK

comprises an intricate network of valleys, forests, and canyons. Located in the southern Sierra Nevada Mountains in the Fresno and Tulare counties of California, it offers diverse terrain, including some of the steepest peaks in the country.

DATE OF VISIT _____

WHERE DID YOU STAY? _____

_____

_____

WHO WERE YOU WITH? _____

_____

_____

WHAT DID YOU DO? _____

_____

_____

_____

WHAT DID YOU SEE? _____

_____

_____

_____

FLORA _____

_____

FAUNA _____

_____

FAVORITE MEMORIES _____

_____

_____

_____

_____

_____

_____

_____

_____

ATTRACTIONS VISITED

- [ ] Giant Forest
- [ ] Kings Canyon
- [ ] Moro Rock Trail
- [ ] General Sherman Tree
- [ ] Congress Trail

LASSEN VOLCANIC NATIONAL PARK

offers lakes, meadows, mountain peaks, waterfalls, and volcanoes. With elevations ranging from 5,300 feet to 10,000 feet, it boasts every type of volcano: plug dome, cinder cone, shield, and strata.

DATE OF VISIT _____

WHERE DID YOU STAY? _____

_____

WHO WERE YOU WITH? _____

_____

_____

_____

WHAT DID YOU DO? _____

_____

_____

_____

WHAT DID YOU SEE? _____

_____

_____

FLORA _____

_____

FAUNA _____

_____

FAVORITE MEMORIES _____

_____

_____

_____

_____

_____

_____

ATTRACTIONS VISITED

- [ ] Mount Lassen
- [ ] Bumpass Hell
- [ ] Manzanita Lake
- [ ] Cinder Cone Trail
- [ ] Mill Creek Falls

LASSEN VOLCANIC NATIONAL PARK

ESTABLISHED 1916

PINNACLES NATIONAL PARK

ESTABLISHED 2013

PINNACLES NATIONAL PARK

is in Monterey County on the California coast, inland
from Big Sur. It offers exhilarating sights at every
elevation, with cave systems below and high spires
above—the latter of which are the remains of an
eroded volcano.

DATE OF VISIT

WHERE DID YOU STAY?

WHO WERE YOU WITH?

ATTRACTIONS VISITED

- [ ] Bear Gulch Reservoir
- [ ] High Peaks Trail
- [ ] Balconies Caves
- [ ] Condor Gulch Overlook
- [ ] Chalone Peak Trail

WHAT DID YOU DO?

WHAT DID YOU SEE?

FLORA

FAUNA

FAVORITE MEMORIES

REDWOOD NATIONAL PARK

grows nearly half of the redwoods in the world, many of them more than 2,000 years old. The interconnected ecosystem maintains not only the world's largest trees, but also prairies, streams, rivers, and rich natural woodlands.

DATE OF VISIT _____

WHERE DID YOU STAY? _____

_____

_____

ATTRACTIONS VISITED

☐ Tall Trees Grove

☐ Enderts Beach

WHO WERE YOU WITH? _____

☐ California Coastal Trail

_____

☐ Fern Canyon

_____

☐ Stout Grove

WHAT DID YOU DO? _____

_____

_____

_____

WHAT DID YOU SEE? _____

_____

_____

FLORA _____

FAUNA _____

FAVORITE MEMORIES _____

_____

_____

_____

_____

_____

_____

_____

REDWOOD NATIONAL PARK

ESTABLISHED 1968

YOSEMITE NATIONAL PARK

ESTABLISHED 1890

YOSEMITE NATIONAL PARK

is famed for its giant sequoia trees and has inspired generations of artists, writers, and politicians. It's impossible to experience this exquisite land without feeling a yearning to connect deeper to the natural treasures of California.

DATE OF VISIT _____

WHERE DID YOU STAY? _____

_____

_____

WHO WERE YOU WITH? _____

_____

_____

WHAT DID YOU DO? _____

_____

_____

_____

WHAT DID YOU SEE? _____

_____

_____

FLORA _____

_____

FAUNA _____

_____

FAVORITE MEMORIES _____

_____

_____

_____

_____

_____

ATTRACTIONS VISITED

- ☐ Mariposa Grove of Giant Sequoias
- ☐ Tunnel View
- ☐ Four Mile Trail
- ☐ Yosemite Village
- ☐ Teolumne Meadows

SEQUOIA NATIONAL PARK

boasts the tallest peak in North America and houses groves of colossal sequoia trees in the belly of California. With an extensive underground cave system, there is as much to explore underground as on the surface.

DATE OF VISIT _____

WHERE DID YOU STAY? _____

_____

WHO WERE YOU WITH? _____

_____

_____

WHAT DID YOU DO? _____

_____

_____

_____

WHAT DID YOU SEE? _____

_____

_____

FLORA _____

FAUNA _____

FAVORITE MEMORIES _____

_____

_____

_____

_____

_____

_____

ATTRACTIONS VISITED

- [ ] Crystal Cave
- [ ] Tunnel Log
- [ ] Grant Grove
- [ ] General Grant Tree Trail
- [ ] Generals Highway Scenic Drive

SEQUOIA NATIONAL PARK

ESTABLISHED 1890

ARCHES NATIONAL PARK

ESTABLISHED 1929

ARCHES NATIONAL PARK

With 2,000 naturally occurring arches, Arches National Park is located just four miles north of the town of Moab in southwestern Utah. It spans 120 square miles and reaches an elevation of 5,653 feet.

DATE OF VISIT

WHERE DID YOU STAY?

WHO WERE YOU WITH?

ATTRACTIONS VISITED

☐ Delicate Arch
☐ Devil's Garden Trailhead
☐ Fiery Furnace
☐ Double Arch
☐ Sand Dune Arch

WHAT DID YOU DO?

WHAT DID YOU SEE?

FLORA

FAUNA

FAVORITE MEMORIES

CAPITOL REEF NATIONAL PARK

is named for the nautical term *reef*, meaning "barrier to passage." Greenery and gentle streams can be found alongside towering canyons, monoliths, and ridges.

DATE OF VISIT _____

WHERE DID YOU STAY? _____

_____

_____

WHO WERE YOU WITH? _____

_____

_____

_____

ATTRACTIONS VISITED

☐ The Hickman Bridge Trail

☐ Cassidy Arch

☐ Capitol Gorge Trail

☐ Fremont Petroglyphs

☐ Goosenecks Overlook

WHAT DID YOU DO? _____

_____

_____

_____

WHAT DID YOU SEE? _____

_____

_____

FLORA _____

FAUNA _____

FAVORITE MEMORIES _____

_____

_____

_____

_____

_____

_____

CAPITOL REEF NATIONAL PARK

ESTABLISHED 1971

ZION NATIONAL PARK

is situated at the intersection of the Mojave Desert, the Great Basin, and the Colorado Plateau. Formed by mesas, monoliths, buttes, arches, and canyons, it is a metropolis of animal life, with 289 bird species and 79 species of mammal.

DATE OF VISIT _____

WHERE DID YOU STAY? _____

_____

_____

ATTRACTIONS VISITED
- [ ] The Narrows
- [ ] Angels Landing
- [ ] Observation Point
- [ ] Emerald Pools Trail
- [ ] Kolob Canyons

WHO WERE YOU WITH? _____

_____

WHAT DID YOU DO? _____

_____

_____

_____

WHAT DID YOU SEE? _____

_____

_____

FLORA _____

FAUNA _____

FAVORITE MEMORIES _____

_____

_____

_____

_____

_____

_____

_____

CANYONLANDS NATIONAL PARK

is separated into four distinct districts: the Island in the Sky, the Needles, the Maze, and the Green & Colorado Rivers. Tributaries and rivers eroded the canyons, mesas, and buttes that make up its 337,598 acres.

DATE OF VISIT _____

WHERE DID YOU STAY? _____

_____

_____

WHO WERE YOU WITH? _____

_____

_____

_____

ATTRACTIONS VISITED
- ☐ Mesa Arch
- ☐ Island in the Sky
- ☐ Grand View Point Overlook
- ☐ The Needles
- ☐ Shafer Trail

WHAT DID YOU DO? _____

_____

_____

_____

WHAT DID YOU SEE? _____

_____

_____

FLORA _____

_____

FAUNA _____

_____

FAVORITE MEMORIES _____

_____

_____

_____

_____

_____

_____

_____

CANYONLANDS NATIONAL PARK

ESTABLISHED 1964

GREAT BASIN NATIONAL PARK

ESTABLISHED 1986

GREAT BASIN NATIONAL PARK

is located in eastern Nevada along the Utah border and protects 77,000 acres of multifarious desert landscape bordered by soaring mountain ranges.

DATE OF VISIT _____

WHERE DID YOU STAY? _____

_____

_____

WHO WERE YOU WITH? _____

ATTRACTIONS VISITED

☐ Wheeler Peak
☐ Bristlecone Trails
☐ Lehman Caves
☐ Teresa Lake
☐ Alpine Lakes Loop

WHAT DID YOU DO? _____

WHAT DID YOU SEE? _____

FLORA _____

FAUNA _____

FAVORITE MEMORIES _____

MOUNT RAINIER NATIONAL PARK

is a colossal, snow-drizzled behemoth of a mountain in western Washington State. The park's idyllic beauty is almost enough to make visitors forget that the mountain is an active stratovolcano and is one of the most dangerous volcanoes in the world.

DATE OF VISIT _____

WHERE DID YOU STAY? _____

_____

_____

ATTRACTIONS VISITED
- ☐ Skyline Trail
- ☐ Grove of the Patriachs
- ☐ Paradise Loop
- ☐ Narada Falls
- ☐ Tipsoo Lake Loop

WHO WERE YOU WITH? _____

_____

_____

WHAT DID YOU DO? _____

_____

_____

_____

WHAT DID YOU SEE? _____

_____

_____

_____

FLORA _____

_____

FAUNA _____

_____

FAVORITE MEMORIES _____

_____

_____

_____

_____

_____

_____

MOUNT RAINIER NATIONAL PARK

ESTABLISHED 1899

NORTH CASCADES NATIONAL PARK

ESTABLISHED 1968

NORTH CASCADES NATIONAL PARK

is a diverse region, with snowy mountain tops on one end, and waterfalls and gushing whitewater on the other. Mountains and glaciers surround the over 500,000 acres of preserved wilderness, with peaks just cresting over 9,000 feet.

DATE OF VISIT _____

WHERE DID YOU STAY? _____

_____

_____

WHO WERE YOU WITH? _____

_____

_____

WHAT DID YOU DO? _____

_____

_____

_____

WHAT DID YOU SEE? _____

_____

_____

FLORA _____

FAUNA _____

FAVORITE MEMORIES _____

_____

_____

_____

_____

_____

_____

_____

ATTRACTIONS VISITED

- ☐ Washington Pass Overlook
- ☐ Diablo Lake Overlook
- ☐ Maple Pass Loop
- ☐ Cascade Pass
- ☐ North Cascades Highway

OLYMPIC NATIONAL PARK

is uniquely coniferous from the large amounts of rainfall and cold waters of the Pacific. Located in the northwest corner of Washington State, it encompasses nearly a million acres, including the transcendent Olympic Mountains.

DATE OF VISIT _____

WHERE DID YOU STAY? _____

_____

_____

WHO WERE YOU WITH? _____

_____

_____

ATTRACTIONS VISITED

☐ Sol Duc Falls

☐ Hoh Rain Forest

☐ Hurricane Ridge

☐ Ruby Beach

☐ Lake Crescent

WHAT DID YOU DO? _____

_____

_____

_____

WHAT DID YOU SEE? _____

_____

_____

FLORA _____

_____

FAUNA _____

_____

FAVORITE MEMORIES _____

_____

_____

_____

_____

_____

_____

OLYMPIC NATIONAL PARK

ESTABLISHED 1938

CRATER LAKE NATIONAL PARK

ESTABLISHED 1902

CRATER LAKE NATIONAL PARK

is a caldera formed by the eruption of the now-defunct volcano Mount Mazama. Located in southwest Oregon, it is the deepest lake in the United States, with an astonishing shade of cobalt blue formed from rain and snow.

DATE OF VISIT _____

WHERE DID YOU STAY? _____

_____

WHO WERE YOU WITH? _____

_____

ATTRACTIONS VISITED
- ☐ Crater Lake
- ☐ Toketee Falls
- ☐ Cleetwood Cove Trail
- ☐ Rim Drive
- ☐ Wizard Island

WHAT DID YOU DO? _____

_____

_____

_____

WHAT DID YOU SEE? _____

_____

_____

FLORA _____

FAUNA _____

FAVORITE MEMORIES _____

_____

_____

_____

_____

_____

_____

DENALI NATIONAL PARK

sits in Alaska and is larger than the entire state of New Hampshire. Filled with treacherous mountains, slippery glaciers, and 350 grizzlies who call this park home, it is not the most easily traversed.

DATE OF VISIT _____

WHERE DID YOU STAY? _____

_____

WHO WERE YOU WITH? _____

_____

_____

_____

WHAT DID YOU DO? _____

_____

_____

_____

WHAT DID YOU SEE? _____

_____

_____

FLORA _____

FAUNA _____

FAVORITE MEMORIES _____

_____

_____

_____

_____

_____

_____

ATTRACTIONS VISITED

- [ ] Mt. Healy Overlook Trail
- [ ] Savage Alpine Trail
- [ ] Horseshoe Lake Trail
- [ ] Wonder Lake
- [ ] Husky Homestead

DENALI NATIONAL PARK

ESTABLISHED 1917.

GATES OF THE ARCTIC NATIONAL PARK

ESTABLISHED 1980

GATES OF THE ARTIC NATIONAL PARK

is the most remote park in the country, located in northern Alaska. It is stationed far above the Arctic Circle and includes 8.4 million acres of snow-blasted mountains, undulating sand dunes, and lively forests.

DATE OF VISIT

WHERE DID YOU STAY?

WHO WERE YOU WITH?

ATTRACTIONS VISITED
- [ ] Koyukuk River
- [ ] John River
- [ ] Arrigetch Peaks
- [ ] Mount Igikpak
- [ ] Takahula Lake

WHAT DID YOU DO?

WHAT DID YOU SEE?

FLORA

FAUNA

FAVORITE MEMORIES

GLACIER BAY NATIONAL PARK

showcases the beauty of Alaska's mountains, fjords, and glaciers. In the islands of the Alexander Archipelago in southeast Alaska, bears, lynx, and wolverines call the park's inlets and islands home, with whales claiming the bay.

DATE OF VISIT _____

WHERE DID YOU STAY? _____

_____

_____

WHO WERE YOU WITH? _____

_____

_____

WHAT DID YOU DO? _____

_____

_____

_____

WHAT DID YOU SEE? _____

_____

_____

FLORA _____

_____

FAUNA _____

_____

FAVORITE MEMORIES _____

_____

_____

_____

_____

_____

_____

ATTRACTIONS VISITED

- ☐ Mount Fairweather
- ☐ Margerie Glacier
- ☐ Bartlett Cove
- ☐ Johns Hopkins Glacier
- ☐ Lituya Bay

GLACIER BAY NATIONAL PARK

ESTABLISHED 1980

KATMAI NATIONAL PARK

ESTABLISHED 1980

KATMAI NATIONAL PARK

lies at the base of Alaska's southern peninsula, 200 miles from Anchorage. Infamous for its 1912 volcanic eruption of Novarupta—the largest of the twentieth century—life continues to reclaim the land.

DATE OF VISIT _____

WHERE DID YOU STAY? _____

_____

_____

ATTRACTIONS VISITED

☐ Brooks River and Falls

WHO WERE YOU WITH? _____

☐ Naknek Lake

☐ Baked Mountain

_____

☐ Savonoski Loop

_____

☐ Valley of Ten
Thousand Smokes

WHAT DID YOU DO? _____

_____

_____

_____

WHAT DID YOU SEE? _____

_____

_____

FLORA _____

FAUNA _____

FAVORITE MEMORIES _____

_____

_____

_____

_____

_____

_____

KENAI FJORDS NATIONAL PARK

is a blinding white expanse of ice and ocean, with forty glaciers carving out the serrated coastline at the base of Alaska's southern peninsula. Meanwhile, the wilderness is lush and green, offering a diverse landscape.

DATE OF VISIT _____

WHERE DID YOU STAY? _____

_____

WHO WERE YOU WITH? _____

_____

_____

_____

ATTRACTIONS VISITED

☐ Exit Glacier

☐ Fox Island

☐ Six Mile Creek

☐ Harding Icefield Trail

☐ Pedersen Glacier

WHAT DID YOU DO? _____

_____

_____

_____

WHAT DID YOU SEE? _____

_____

_____

FLORA _____

_____

FAUNA _____

_____

FAVORITE MEMORIES _____

_____

_____

_____

_____

_____

_____

KENAI FJORDS NATIONAL PARK

ESTABLISHED 1980

KOBUK VALLEY NATIONAL PARK

ESTABLISHED 1980

KOBUK VALLEY NATIONAL PARK

is one of the most remote wilderness preserves in the country, spread over more than two million acres of wilderness in upper Alaska, smack in the middle of the arctic tundra and inhabited by caribou and native Eskimo.

VISITOR'S STAMP

DATE OF VISIT _____

WHERE DID YOU STAY? _____

ATTRACTIONS VISITED

- [ ] Great Kobuk Sand Dunes
- [ ] Baird Mountains
- [ ] Kobuk River
- [ ] Northwest Arctic Heritage Center
- [ ] Hunt River Sand Dunes

WHO WERE YOU WITH? _____

WHAT DID YOU DO? _____

WHAT DID YOU SEE? _____

FLORA _____

FAUNA _____

FAVORITE MEMORIES _____

LAKE CLARK NATIONAL PARK

is only accessible by boat or by float plane. It got its name from a forty-mile-long and five-mile-wide pool of fresh teal water, surrounded by mountains, volcanoes, glaciers, prairies, bogs, and shoreline.

DATE OF VISIT _____

WHERE DID YOU STAY? _____
_____
_____

WHO WERE YOU WITH? _____
_____
_____
_____

ATTRACTIONS VISITED

- [ ] Turquoise Lake
- [ ] Kontrashibuna Lake
- [ ] Chilikadrotna River
- [ ] Tanalian Falls Trailhead
- [ ] Tlikakila River

WHAT DID YOU DO? _____
_____
_____
_____

WHAT DID YOU SEE? _____
_____
_____

FLORA _____
_____

FAUNA _____
_____

FAVORITE MEMORIES _____
_____
_____
_____
_____
_____
_____

LAKE CLARK NATIONAL PARK

ESTABLISHED 1980

WRANGELL–ST. ELIAS NATIONAL PARK

ESTABLISHED 1980

WRANGELL—ST. ELIAS NATIONAL PARK

is the largest national park in the US. Surrounded by imposing mountain ranges, it offers the most glaciers, the most Dall sheep, the largest grizzly bears, and the highest peaks of any park or preserve in the country.

DATE OF VISIT _____

WHERE DID YOU STAY? _____

_____

_____

WHO WERE YOU WITH? _____

_____

_____

ATTRACTIONS VISITED

- ☐ Root Glacier Trail
- ☐ Mount Blackburn
- ☐ Nabesna Road
- ☐ Rambler Mine Trail
- ☐ Kennecott Copper Mine

WHAT DID YOU DO? _____

_____

_____

_____

WHAT DID YOU SEE? _____

_____

_____

FLORA _____

FAUNA _____

FAVORITE MEMORIES _____

_____

_____

_____

_____

_____

_____

CHANNEL ISLANDS NATIONAL PARK

is an archipelago of five islands just offshore from California. Anacapa, Santa Barbara, Santa Cruz, San Miguel, and Santa Rosa are biosphere reserves and provide stunning sights, sounds, and sensations.

DATE OF VISIT

WHERE DID YOU STAY?

WHO WERE YOU WITH?

WHAT DID YOU DO?

WHAT DID YOU SEE?

FLORA

FAUNA

FAVORITE MEMORIES

ATTRACTIONS VISITED
- [ ] Channel Islands
- [ ] The Sea Caves
- [ ] Painted Cave
- [ ] Potato Harbor Road
- [ ] Scorpion Anchorage

STATE: CALIFORNIA | ARTIST: SOPHIE DIAO

CHANNEL ISLANDS NATIONAL PARK

ESTABLISHED 1980

HALEAKALĀ NATIONAL PARK

ESTABLISHED 1961

HALEAKALĀ NATIONAL PARK

consists of five square miles of land in Hawaii that surround a defunct volcano, dotted with craters, cinder cones, and volcanic phenomenon.

DATE OF VISIT _____

WHERE DID YOU STAY? _____
_____
_____

WHO WERE YOU WITH? _____
_____
_____

WHAT DID YOU DO? _____
_____
_____
_____

WHAT DID YOU SEE? _____
_____
_____

FLORA _____

FAUNA _____

FAVORITE MEMORIES _____
_____
_____
_____
_____
_____
_____

ATTRACTIONS VISITED
- ☐ Haleakalā Crater
- ☐ Sliding Sands Trail
- ☐ Pipiwai Trail
- ☐ 'Ohe'o Gulch

HAWAII VOLCANOES NATIONAL PARK

contains two volcanoes: Mauna Loa, which stands
13,679 feet high as the world's largest shield volcano;
and Mount Kilauea, which stands 4,091 feet tall as the
world's most active volcano.

DATE OF VISIT _____

WHERE DID YOU STAY? _____

_____

_____

_____

WHO WERE YOU WITH? _____

_____

_____

_____

WHAT DID YOU DO? _____

_____

_____

WHAT DID YOU SEE? _____

_____

_____

FLORA _____

_____

FAUNA _____

_____

FAVORITE MEMORIES _____

_____

_____

_____

_____

_____

_____

_____

VISITOR'S STAMP

ATTRACTIONS VISITED

- ☐ Nahuku-Thurston Lava Tube
- ☐ Kīlauea Iki Trail
- ☐ Hōlei Sea Arch
- ☐ Kipuka Puaulu (Bird Park) Trail
- ☐ Puʻu Loa Petroglyphs

STATE: HAWAII   ARTIST: VINCENT ROCHE

HAWAII VOLCANOES NATIONAL PARK

ESTABLISHED 1916

NATIONAL PARK OF AMERICAN SAMOA

ESTABLISHED 1988

NATIONAL PARK OF AMERICAN SAMOA

offers an array of tropical biodiversity ranging from mountains and volcanoes to coral reefs and rainforests. Situated along three Oceanic islands, tide pools and sparkling waterfalls accent the beauty of this tropical paradise.

DATE OF VISIT _____

WHERE DID YOU STAY? _____

_____

_____

ATTRACTIONS VISITED

☐ Mount 'Alava

☐ Two Dollar Beach

WHO WERE YOU WITH? _____

☐ Lower Sauma Ridge Hike

☐ Matafao Peak

_____

☐ Ofu Beach

_____

WHAT DID YOU DO? _____

_____

_____

_____

WHAT DID YOU SEE? _____

_____

_____

FLORA _____

_____

FAUNA _____

_____

FAVORITE MEMORIES _____

_____

_____

_____

_____

_____

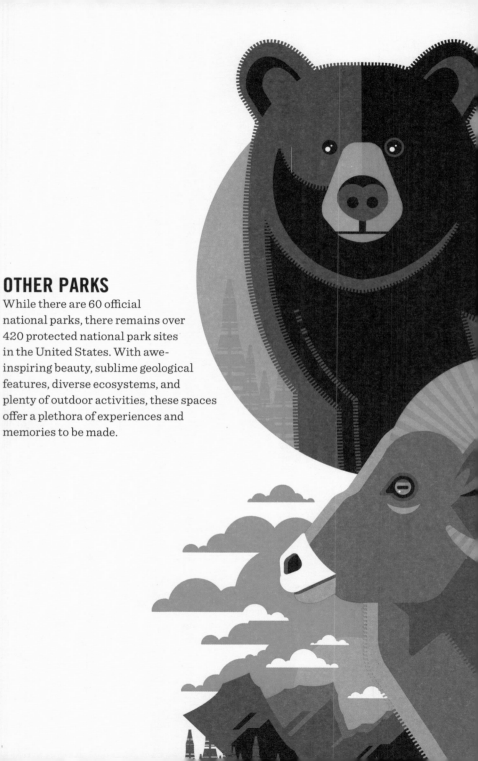

OTHER PARKS

While there are 60 official national parks, there remains over 420 protected national park sites in the United States. With awe-inspiring beauty, sublime geological features, diverse ecosystems, and plenty of outdoor activities, these spaces offer a plethora of experiences and memories to be made.

PARK NAME _____

DATE OF VISIT _____

WHERE DID YOU STAY? _____
_____
_____

WHO WERE YOU WITH? _____
_____
_____

WHAT DID YOU DO? _____
_____
_____
_____

WHAT DID YOU SEE? _____
_____
_____

FLORA _____
_____

FAUNA _____
_____

FAVORITE MEMORIES _____
_____
_____
_____
_____
_____
_____
_____
_____
_____
_____

VISITOR'S STAMP

ATTRACTIONS VISITED
☐
☐
☐
☐
☐

PARK NAME

DATE OF VISIT

WHERE DID YOU STAY?

WHO WERE YOU WITH?

WHAT DID YOU DO?

WHAT DID YOU SEE?

FLORA

FAUNA

FAVORITE MEMORIES

ATTRACTIONS VISITED

☐
☐
☐
☐
☐

PARK NAME

DATE OF VISIT

WHERE DID YOU STAY?

WHO WERE YOU WITH?

WHAT DID YOU DO?

WHAT DID YOU SEE?

FLORA

FAUNA

FAVORITE MEMORIES

VISITOR'S STAMP

ATTRACTIONS VISITED
- [ ]
- [ ]
- [ ]
- [ ]
- [ ]

PARK NAME _____

DATE OF VISIT _____

WHERE DID YOU STAY? _____
_____
_____

WHO WERE YOU WITH? _____
_____
_____

WHAT DID YOU DO? _____
_____
_____
_____

WHAT DID YOU SEE? _____
_____
_____

FLORA _____
_____

FAUNA _____
_____

FAVORITE MEMORIES _____
_____
_____
_____
_____
_____
_____
_____
_____
_____
_____

VISITOR'S STAMP

ATTRACTIONS VISITED
- ☐
- ☐
- ☐
- ☐
- ☐

PARK NAME _____

DATE OF VISIT _____

WHERE DID YOU STAY? _____
_____
_____

WHO WERE YOU WITH? _____
_____
_____

WHAT DID YOU DO? _____
_____
_____
_____

WHAT DID YOU SEE? _____
_____
_____

FLORA _____
_____

FAUNA _____
_____

FAVORITE MEMORIES _____
_____
_____
_____
_____
_____
_____
_____
_____
_____
_____

VISITOR'S STAMP

ATTRACTIONS VISITED
☐
☐
☐
☐
☐

PARK NAME

DATE OF VISIT

WHERE DID YOU STAY?

WHO WERE YOU WITH?

WHAT DID YOU DO?

WHAT DID YOU SEE?

FLORA

FAUNA

FAVORITE MEMORIES

VISITOR'S STAMP

ATTRACTIONS VISITED
- [ ]
- [ ]
- [ ]
- [ ]
- [ ]

PARK NAME _____

DATE OF VISIT _____

WHERE DID YOU STAY? _____
_____
_____

WHO WERE YOU WITH? _____
_____
_____

WHAT DID YOU DO? _____
_____
_____
_____

WHAT DID YOU SEE? _____
_____
_____

FLORA _____
_____

FAUNA _____
_____

FAVORITE MEMORIES _____
_____
_____
_____
_____
_____
_____
_____
_____
_____
_____

VISITOR'S STAMP

ATTRACTIONS VISITED
- ☐
- ☐
- ☐
- ☐
- ☐

PARK NAME _____

DATE OF VISIT _____

WHERE DID YOU STAY? _____
_____
_____

WHO WERE YOU WITH? _____
_____

WHAT DID YOU DO? _____
_____
_____
_____

WHAT DID YOU SEE? _____
_____
_____

FLORA _____
_____

FAUNA _____
_____

FAVORITE MEMORIES _____
_____
_____
_____
_____
_____
_____
_____
_____
_____
_____
_____

VISITOR'S STAMP

ATTRACTIONS VISITED
- ☐
- ☐
- ☐
- ☐
- ☐

PARK NAME _____

DATE OF VISIT _____

WHERE DID YOU STAY? _____

_____

_____

WHO WERE YOU WITH? _____

_____

_____

WHAT DID YOU DO? _____

_____

_____

_____

WHAT DID YOU SEE? _____

_____

_____

FLORA _____

FAUNA _____

FAVORITE MEMORIES _____

_____

_____

_____

_____

_____

_____

_____

_____

_____

_____

VISITOR'S STAMP

ATTRACTIONS VISITED

☐
☐
☐
☐
☐

146

PARK NAME _____

DATE OF VISIT _____

WHERE DID YOU STAY? _____
_____
_____

WHO WERE YOU WITH? _____
_____
_____

WHAT DID YOU DO? _____
_____
_____
_____

WHAT DID YOU SEE? _____
_____
_____

FLORA _____
_____

FAUNA _____
_____

FAVORITE MEMORIES _____
_____
_____
_____
_____
_____
_____
_____
_____
_____
_____
_____

VISITOR'S STAMP

ATTRACTIONS VISITED

☐
☐
☐
☐
☐

PARK NAME _____

DATE OF VISIT _____

WHERE DID YOU STAY? _____
_____
_____

WHO WERE YOU WITH? _____
_____
_____

WHAT DID YOU DO? _____
_____
_____
_____

WHAT DID YOU SEE? _____
_____
_____

FLORA _____
_____

FAUNA _____
_____

FAVORITE MEMORIES _____
_____
_____
_____
_____
_____
_____
_____
_____
_____
_____
_____

VISITOR'S STAMP

ATTRACTIONS VISITED
- [ ]
- [ ]
- [ ]
- [ ]
- [ ]

PARK NAME _____

DATE OF VISIT _____

WHERE DID YOU STAY? _____

_____

_____

WHO WERE YOU WITH? _____

_____

_____

WHAT DID YOU DO? _____

_____

_____

_____

WHAT DID YOU SEE? _____

_____

_____

FLORA _____

_____

FAUNA _____

_____

FAVORITE MEMORIES _____

_____

_____

_____

_____

_____

_____

_____

_____

_____

_____

VISITOR'S STAMP

ATTRACTIONS VISITED

- [ ]
- [ ]
- [ ]
- [ ]
- [ ]

PARK NAME _____

DATE OF VISIT _____

WHERE DID YOU STAY? _____

_____

_____

WHO WERE YOU WITH? _____

_____

_____

WHAT DID YOU DO? _____

_____

_____

_____

WHAT DID YOU SEE? _____

_____

_____

FLORA _____

_____

FAUNA _____

_____

FAVORITE MEMORIES _____

_____

_____

_____

_____

_____

_____

_____

_____

_____

_____

_____

_____

_____

VISITOR'S STAMP

ATTRACTIONS VISITED
- [ ]
- [ ]
- [ ]
- [ ]
- [ ]

PARK NAME _____

DATE OF VISIT _____

WHERE DID YOU STAY? _____
_____
_____

WHO WERE YOU WITH? _____
_____

WHAT DID YOU DO? _____
_____
_____
_____

WHAT DID YOU SEE? _____
_____
_____

FLORA _____

FAUNA _____

FAVORITE MEMORIES _____
_____
_____
_____
_____
_____
_____
_____
_____
_____
_____
_____

VISITOR'S STAMP

ATTRACTIONS VISITED
- ☐
- ☐
- ☐
- ☐
- ☐

PARK NAME _____

DATE OF VISIT _____

WHERE DID YOU STAY? _____
_____
_____

WHO WERE YOU WITH? _____
_____
_____

WHAT DID YOU DO? _____
_____
_____
_____

WHAT DID YOU SEE? _____
_____
_____

FLORA _____

FAUNA _____

FAVORITE MEMORIES _____
_____
_____
_____
_____
_____
_____
_____
_____
_____
_____

VISITOR'S STAMP

ATTRACTIONS VISITED
- [ ]
- [ ]
- [ ]
- [ ]
- [ ]

PARK NAME _____

DATE OF VISIT _____

WHERE DID YOU STAY? _____
_____
_____

WHO WERE YOU WITH? _____
_____
_____

WHAT DID YOU DO? _____
_____
_____
_____

WHAT DID YOU SEE? _____
_____
_____

FLORA _____

FAUNA _____

FAVORITE MEMORIES _____
_____
_____
_____
_____
_____
_____
_____
_____
_____
_____
_____

VISITOR'S STAMP

ATTRACTIONS VISITED
☐
☐
☐
☐
☐

PARK NAME _____

DATE OF VISIT _____

WHERE DID YOU STAY? _____

WHO WERE YOU WITH? _____

WHAT DID YOU DO? _____

WHAT DID YOU SEE? _____

FLORA _____

FAUNA _____

FAVORITE MEMORIES _____

_____

_____

_____

_____

_____

_____

_____

_____

_____

_____

_____

VISITOR'S STAMP

ATTRACTIONS VISITED
- [ ]
- [ ]
- [ ]
- [ ]
- [ ]

PARK NAME _____

DATE OF VISIT _____

WHERE DID YOU STAY? _____
_____
_____

WHO WERE YOU WITH? _____
_____
_____

WHAT DID YOU DO? _____
_____
_____
_____

WHAT DID YOU SEE? _____
_____
_____
_____

FLORA _____
_____

FAUNA _____
_____

FAVORITE MEMORIES _____
_____
_____
_____
_____
_____
_____
_____
_____
_____
_____

VISITOR'S STAMP

ATTRACTIONS VISITED
- ☐
- ☐
- ☐
- ☐
- ☐

PARK NAME _____

DATE OF VISIT _____

WHERE DID YOU STAY? _____
_____
_____

WHO WERE YOU WITH? _____
_____
_____

WHAT DID YOU DO? _____
_____
_____
_____

WHAT DID YOU SEE? _____
_____
_____

FLORA _____
_____

FAUNA _____
_____

FAVORITE MEMORIES _____
_____
_____
_____
_____
_____
_____
_____
_____
_____
_____

VISITOR'S STAMP

ATTRACTIONS VISITED
- [ ]
- [ ]
- [ ]
- [ ]
- [ ]

PARK NAME _____

DATE OF VISIT _____

WHERE DID YOU STAY? _____

_____

_____

WHO WERE YOU WITH? _____

_____

_____

WHAT DID YOU DO? _____

_____

_____

_____

WHAT DID YOU SEE? _____

_____

_____

FLORA _____

_____

FAUNA _____

_____

FAVORITE MEMORIES _____

_____

_____

_____

_____

_____

_____

_____

_____

_____

_____

VISITOR'S STAMP

ATTRACTIONS VISITED

- [ ]
- [ ]
- [ ]
- [ ]
- [ ]

PARK NAME _____

DATE OF VISIT _____

WHERE DID YOU STAY? _____
_____
_____

WHO WERE YOU WITH? _____
_____

WHAT DID YOU DO? _____
_____
_____
_____

WHAT DID YOU SEE? _____
_____
_____

FLORA _____
_____

FAUNA _____
_____

FAVORITE MEMORIES _____
_____
_____
_____
_____
_____
_____
_____
_____
_____

VISITOR'S STAMP

ATTRACTIONS VISITED
- ☐
- ☐
- ☐
- ☐
- ☐

PARK NAME _____

DATE OF VISIT _____

WHERE DID YOU STAY? _____
_____
_____

WHO WERE YOU WITH? _____
_____
_____

WHAT DID YOU DO? _____
_____
_____
_____

WHAT DID YOU SEE? _____
_____
_____

FLORA _____
_____

FAUNA _____
_____

FAVORITE MEMORIES _____
_____
_____
_____
_____
_____
_____
_____
_____
_____
_____
_____

VISITOR'S STAMP

ATTRACTIONS VISITED

☐
☐
☐
☐
☐

PARK NAME _____

DATE OF VISIT _____

WHERE DID YOU STAY? _____
_____
_____

WHO WERE YOU WITH? _____
_____
_____

WHAT DID YOU DO? _____
_____
_____
_____

WHAT DID YOU SEE? _____
_____
_____

FLORA _____
_____

FAUNA _____
_____

FAVORITE MEMORIES _____
_____
_____
_____
_____
_____
_____
_____
_____
_____
_____

VISITOR'S STAMP

ATTRACTIONS VISITED
☐
☐
☐
☐
☐

PARK NAME _____

DATE OF VISIT _____

WHERE DID YOU STAY? _____
_____
_____

WHO WERE YOU WITH? _____
_____

WHAT DID YOU DO? _____
_____
_____
_____

WHAT DID YOU SEE? _____
_____
_____

FLORA _____

FAUNA _____

FAVORITE MEMORIES _____
_____
_____
_____
_____
_____
_____
_____
_____
_____

VISITOR'S STAMP

ATTRACTIONS VISITED
- [ ]
- [ ]
- [ ]
- [ ]
- [ ]

PARK NAME _____

DATE OF VISIT _____

WHERE DID YOU STAY? _____
_____
_____

WHO WERE YOU WITH? _____
_____
_____

WHAT DID YOU DO? _____
_____
_____
_____

WHAT DID YOU SEE? _____
_____
_____

FLORA _____
_____

FAUNA _____
_____

FAVORITE MEMORIES _____
_____
_____
_____
_____
_____
_____
_____
_____
_____
_____
_____

ATTRACTIONS VISITED
- ☐
- ☐
- ☐
- ☐
- ☐

PARK NAME

DATE OF VISIT

WHERE DID YOU STAY?

WHO WERE YOU WITH?

WHAT DID YOU DO?

WHAT DID YOU SEE?

FLORA

FAUNA

FAVORITE MEMORIES

VISITOR'S STAMP

ATTRACTIONS VISITED
- [ ]
- [ ]
- [ ]
- [ ]
- [ ]

PARK NAME _____

DATE OF VISIT _____

WHERE DID YOU STAY? _____
_____
_____

WHO WERE YOU WITH? _____
_____
_____

WHAT DID YOU DO? _____
_____
_____
_____

WHAT DID YOU SEE? _____
_____
_____

FLORA _____

FAUNA _____

FAVORITE MEMORIES _____
_____
_____
_____
_____
_____
_____
_____
_____
_____

VISITOR'S STAMP

ATTRACTIONS VISITED
- [ ]
- [ ]
- [ ]
- [ ]
- [ ]

PARK NAME _____

DATE OF VISIT _____

WHERE DID YOU STAY? _____
_____
_____

WHO WERE YOU WITH? _____
_____

WHAT DID YOU DO? _____
_____
_____
_____

WHAT DID YOU SEE? _____
_____
_____

FLORA _____
_____

FAUNA _____
_____

FAVORITE MEMORIES _____
_____
_____
_____
_____
_____
_____
_____
_____
_____
_____

VISITOR'S STAMP

ATTRACTIONS VISITED
☐
☐
☐
☐
☐

PARK NAME

DATE OF VISIT

WHERE DID YOU STAY?

WHO WERE YOU WITH?

WHAT DID YOU DO?

WHAT DID YOU SEE?

FLORA

FAUNA

FAVORITE MEMORIES

VISITOR'S STAMP

ATTRACTIONS VISITED
- [ ]
- [ ]
- [ ]
- [ ]
- [ ]

PARK NAME _____

DATE OF VISIT _____

WHERE DID YOU STAY? _____
_____
_____

WHO WERE YOU WITH? _____
_____

WHAT DID YOU DO? _____
_____
_____
_____

WHAT DID YOU SEE? _____
_____
_____

FLORA _____
_____

FAUNA _____
_____

FAVORITE MEMORIES _____
_____
_____
_____
_____
_____
_____
_____
_____
_____
_____

VISITOR'S STAMP

ATTRACTIONS VISITED
☐
☐
☐
☐
☐

PARK NAME _____

DATE OF VISIT _____

WHERE DID YOU STAY? _____

_____

_____

WHO WERE YOU WITH? _____

_____

_____

WHAT DID YOU DO? _____

_____

_____

_____

WHAT DID YOU SEE? _____

_____

_____

FLORA _____

_____

FAUNA _____

_____

FAVORITE MEMORIES _____

_____

_____

_____

_____

_____

_____

_____

_____

_____

_____

VISITOR'S STAMP

ATTRACTIONS VISITED

☐

☐

☐

☐

☐

INDEX TO NATIONAL PARKS

ABOUT

Fifty-Nine Parks

Fifty-Nine Parks believes that public lands and the art of printmaking are traditions worth preserving. Each of Fifty-Nine Parks' posters are beautifully screen printed in the United States while collaborating with artists from around the world. The poster series is archived by the Library of Congress and proceeds of each poster sale are donated to support the conservation of American public lands. To learn more about the series, please visit 59parks.net.

Fifty-Nine Parks

www.59parks.net

 Find us on Instagram: @fiftynineparks

EARTH AWARE
P.O. Box 3088
San Rafael, CA 94912
www.MandalaEarth.com

Find us on Facebook: www.facebook.com/MandalaEarth
Follow us on Instagram: @MandalaEarth

Publisher: Raoul Goff
Associate Publisher: Roger Shaw
VP of Creative: Chrissy Kwasnik
VP of Manufacturing: Alix Nicholaeff
Associate Art Director: Ashley Quackenbush
Designer: Brooke McCullum
Sponsoring Editor: Matt Wise
Editorial Director: Katie Killebrew
Project Editor: Nicole Crncich
Editorial team: Claire Yee and Sophia Wright
Production Associate: Andy Harper

ISBN: 978-1-64722-582-7

 REPLANTED PAPER

Insight Editions, in association with Roots of Peace, will plant two trees for each tree used in the
manufacturing of this book. Roots of Peace is an internationally renowned humanitarian organization
dedicated to eradicating land mines worldwide and converting war-torn lands into productive farms
and wildlife habitats. Roots of Peace will plant two million fruit and nut trees in Afghanistan and
provide farmers there with the skills and support necessary for sustainable land use.

Manufactured in China

First printed in 2022.

10 9 8 7 6 5